First World War
and Army of Occupation
War Diary
France, Belgium and Germany

57 DIVISION
Headquarters, Branches and Services
Royal Army Medical Corps
Assistant Director Medical Services
1 September 1915 - 29 February 1916

WO95/2969/1

The Naval & Military Press Ltd
www.nmarchive.com
Published in association with The National Archives

Published by

The Naval & Military Press Ltd

Unit 10 Ridgewood Industrial Park,
Uckfield, East Sussex,
TN22 5QE England
Tel: +44 (0) 1825 749494

www.naval-military-press.com
www.nmarchive.com

This diary has been reprinted in facsimile from the original. Any imperfections are inevitably reproduced and the quality may fall short of modern type and cartographic standards.

© **Crown Copyright**
Images reproduced by permission of The National Archives, London, England, 2015.

Contents

Document type	Place/Title	Date From	Date To
Heading	57th Division Asst Dir. Medical Services 1915 Sep-1916 Feb 1917 Feb-1919 Mar		
Heading	WO95/2969/1 Assistant Director Medical Services		
Heading	War Diary and Statement R.A.M.C. Units 1915 Sep October 6th 1915		
War Diary	Canterbury	01/09/1915	30/09/1915
Heading	R.A.M.C. Units, War Diary For The Month Of October 1915		
War Diary	Canterbury	01/10/1915	29/10/1915
Heading	War Diary Of The R.A.M.C. Units 57th (W. Lancs) Div. For The Month Of December 1915		
War Diary	Canterbury	01/12/1915	22/12/1915
Heading	War Diary Of RAMC Units 57th (West Lancs) Divn. From 1st Jany 1916 To 31st Jany 1916		
War Diary	Canterbury	01/01/1916	31/01/1916
Heading	War Diary Of RAMC 57th (West Lancs) Division From 1st Febry 1916 To 29th Feby 1916		
War Diary	Canterbury	11/02/1916	29/02/1916

57TH DIVISION

ASST DIR. MEDICAL SERVICES

~~FEB 1916 - DEC 1918~~

1915 SEP — 1916 FEB.
+
1917 FEB — 1919 MAR

WO95/2469/1

Assistant Director Medical Services

ADMS
4

War Diary and Statement
R.A.M.C. Units

1915 SEP

October 6th 1915.

Army Form C. 2118.

WAR DIARY
or
INTELLIGENCE SUMMARY.
(Erase heading not required.)

Instructions regarding War Diaries and Intelligence Summaries are contained in F. S. Regs., Part II. and the Staff Manual respectively. Title pages will be prepared in manuscript.

Place	Date	Hour	Summary of Events and Information	Remarks and references to Appendices
CANTERBURY.	1/9/15.		A.D.M.S. visited Ashford to inspect a draft of the 2/4th Loyal North Lancs. Regt.	
	2/9/15.		Weekly packing trial carried out by the 1/2nd Field Ambulance. Standing Medical Board assembled at Wye.	
	3/9/15.		Standing Medical Board assembled at Oxted.	
	7/9/15.		War Diary and Statement sent in to Headquarters. Standing Medical Board assembled at Canterbury. 2/1st Field Ambulance carried out Field Exercises at Copthorn.	
	9/9/15.		Weekly packing trial 1/2nd Field Ambulance. Field exercises carried out by 2/1st Field Amblce. Inspection of Medical and Surgical Equipment 4th W.L. Bde. R.F.A., proceeding overseas, carried out by D.A.D.M.S. 57th Division. Standing Medical Board assembled at Oxted Wye.	
	10/9/15.		Inspection of Medical and Surgical Equipment of 2nd & 3rd Brigades R.F.A. proceeding overseas, carried out by D.A.D.M.S. 57th Division. Standing Medical Board assembled at Oxted.	
	11/9/15.		Inspection of Medical and Surgical Equipment of 1st (W.L.) Brigade R.F.A., proceeding overseas, carried out by D.A.D.M.S. 57th Division.	
	14/9/15.		Packing trial and route march carried out by 1/3rd Field Ambulance. Field Exercises carried out by 2/1st Field Ambulance.	
	16/9/15.		Packing trial carried out by 1/2nd Field Ambulance. A.D.M.S. and Sanitary Officer visited Bendridge Camp. 15 Cases of Acute Pharyngitis accompanied by Pyrexia, headache and backache, diagnosed as Influenza admitted to 3rd Field Ambulance.	
	17/9/15.		13 further cases of Influenza admitted to 3rd Field Ambulance.	
	18/9/15. to 21/9/15.		7 further cases of Influenza admitted between the 18th and 21st. All cases have done well. All were found negative to bacteriological examination of swabs from throats.	

Army Form C. 2118.

WAR DIARY
or
INTELLIGENCE SUMMARY.

(Erase heading not required.)

Instructions regarding War Diaries and Intelligence Summaries are contained in F.S. Regs., Part II. and the Staff Manual respectively. Title pages will be prepared in manuscript.

Place	Date	Hour	Summary of Events and Information	Remarks and references to Appendices
CANTERBURY	23/9/15 to 26/9/15		19 Cases of Scabies admitted to 3rd Field Ambulance Reception Hospital.	
	23/9/15.		Night exercises carried out by 3rd Field Ambulance at Chartham Downs. Weekly packing trial 1/2nd Field Ambulance.	
	29/9/15.		A.D.M.S. and D.A.D.M.S. visited dated and inspected 2/1st Field Ambulance.	
	30/9/15		A.D.M.S. 57th Division inspected 1/3rd Field Ambulance at Field Exercises at Hoath.	

CANTERBURY,
6th Oct. 1915.

[signature]
Lt. Col. R.A.M.C.
D.A.D.M.S. for A.D.M.S. 57th (West Lancs) Division.

R.A.M.C. UNITS,

WAR DIARY

for the month of OCTOBER 1915.

Army Form C. 2118

R.A.M Corps
Units

WAR DIARY
or
INTELLIGENCE SUMMARY

(Erase heading not required.)

Instructions regarding War Diaries and Intelligence Summaries are contained in F. S. Regs., Part II. and the Staff Manual respectively. Title Pages will be prepared in manuscript.

Place	Date	Hour	Summary of Events and Information	Remarks and references to Appendices
Canterbury	1.10.15		A.D.M.S. accompanied by D.A.D.M.S. inspected 1/2nd Field Ambulance and Field Ambulance Reception Hospital at Wye. Convoy of wounded, 8 lying down and 12 sitting up taken by 1/3rd Field Ambulance from Canterbury East to Tankerton.	
	5.10.15		D.D.M.S., Central Force visited Canterbury and inspected 1/3rd Field Ambulance the Field Ambulance Reception Hospital at Nackington House and the Isolation Hospital at St. Non's.	
	6.10.15		War Diary and Statement submitted to Headquarters 57th Division.	
	8.10.15		A.D.M.S. and Divisional Sanitary Officer attended Exhibition of Splints and other Surgical War Material at Royal Medical Society, Wimpole Street.	
	9.10.15		Received notification that 1/2nd Field Ambulance have to concentrate at Sheffield. 1/3rd Field Ambulance paraded at Old Park and were addressed by Colonel Romilly with special reference to Munition Workers.	
	14.10.15		Special Medical Board assembled at Crowborough for purpose of examination of men found unfit for service abroad. Lt.Colonel J. D. G. Macpherson R.A.M.C. detailed as President. Convoy of wounded 10 lying and 20 sitting conveyed to Tankerton by 1/3rd Field Ambulance.	
	16.10.15		G.O.C. 57th Division inspected Reception Hospital of the 1/3rd and 1/2nd Field Ambulances at Canterbury and Wye respectively.	
	17.10.15		Captain Lawson R.A.M.C., home from the front gave a lecture to the Field Amb: officers on his experiences at the front.	
	19.10.15.		One section of the 2/1st Field Ambulance proceeded from Oxted to Wye to take over the Reception Hospital of the 1/2nd Field Ambulance under orders for Sheffield.	
	20.10.15.		Advance party of 1/2nd Field Ambulance left Wye for Sheffield.	
	22.10.15.		Main body of 1/2nd Field Ambulance left Wye for Sheffield.	
	25.10.15.		2/1st Field Ambulance left Oxted by route march for Maidstone.	

1875 Wt. W593/826 1,000,000 4/15 J.B.C. & A. A.D.S.S./Forms/C. 2118.

Army Form C. 2118

WAR DIARY
or
INTELLIGENCE SUMMARY

(Erase heading not required.)

Instructions regarding War Diaries and Intelligence Summaries are contained in F. S. Regs., Part II. and the Staff Manual respectively. Title Pages will be prepared in manuscript.

Place	Date	Hour	Summary of Events and Information	Remarks and references to Appendices
Canterbury.	25.10.15.		Night manoeuvres carried out by 1/3rd Field Ambulance.	
	26.10.15.		2/1st Field Ambulance arrived at Maidstone.	
	27.10.15.		Divisional Sanitary Officer visited Sandwich to inspect billets	
	29.10.15.		Drainage at Reception Hospital 1/3rd Field Ambulance (Nackington House) inspected by Divisional Sanitary Officer.	

Canterbury.
6-11-1915.

[signature]

Lt Col. R.A.M.C.
D.A.D.M.S. for A.D.M.S., 57th (West Lancs) Division.

CONFIDENTIAL.

WAR DIARY.

of the
R.A.M.C. Units.
51st (Highland) Div.

for the month of

DECEMBER, 1915.

Army Form C. 2118

WAR DIARY
or
~~INTELLIGENCE SUMMARY~~

(Erase heading not required.)

Instructions regarding War Diaries and Intelligence Summaries are contained in F.S. Regs., Part II. and the Staff Manual respectively. Title Pages will be prepared in manuscript.

Place	Date	Hour	Summary of Events and Information	Remarks and references to Appendices
Canterbury	1/12/15.		Secret letter S.335 received, to Field Ambulance O.C.'s.	
	3/12/15.		Secret letters S. 338 & S.339 received reference moves of two Field Ambulances for service overseas, and of 2/2nd and 2/3rd Wessex Field Ambulances into the Division to fill their places.	
	4/12/15.		Lt.Col. J.D.G. Macpherson D.A.D.M.S. left this Division to report at Aldershot for duty. 2/3rd Wessex Field Ambulance advance party of 1 Officer, 10th OtherRanks arrived at Maidstone 5 p.m. from Bournemouth and party 1 Officer, 10 Other Ranks at Wye from 3/2nd West Lancs. Field Ambulance.	
	5/12/15.		2/3rd Wessex Field Ambulance from 2/2nd Wessex Field Ambulance reported at Canterbury. 2/2nd Wessex Field Ambulance arrived Maidstone, strength 7 Officers, 209 Other Ranks. 3/2nd West Lancs. Field Ambulance arrived Canterbury, strength	
	6/12/15.		2/3rd Wessex Field Ambulance took over Reception Hospital from 2/1st West Lancs Field Ambulance at Maidstone. 3/2nd West Lancs. Field Ambulance took over Reception Hospital and billets of one section of 2/1st West Lancs. Field Ambulance stationed at Wye, Kent. The 2/2nd Wessex Field Ambulance took over Reception Hospital from 1/3rd West Lancs. Field Ambulance under orders for overseas. One section 2 Officer, 25 Other Ranks left Wye to join their unit 2/1st West Lancs. Field Ambulance at Maidstone.	
	7/12/15.		1/3rd West Lancs. Field Ambulance left Canterbury for Salisbury, marching out State 10 Officers 203 Other Ranks leaving behind 20 Munition Workers. 2/1st West Lancs Field Ambulance left Maidstone Marching Out State 5 Officers 178 Other Ranks, 13 Munition Workers left behind.	
	8/12/15.		The A.D.M.S. and Sanitary Officer met D.D.M.S. and Sanitary Officer, Central Force at Wye and Ashford and inspected the 3/2nd West Lancs. Field Ambulance and Reception Hospital, also ward at East Ashford Union Workhouse for patients suffering from Scabies. No patients at Kennington Isolation Camp.	
	9/12/15.		Proceedings of Medical Board on Captain Lockhart received, Finding – Fit for General Service. Captain Edmiston reported for duty as Acting D.A.D.M.S.	
	17/12/15.		A.D.M.S. 57th (W.L.) Division inspected, Personnel, equipment and Reception Hospital of 2/3rd Wessex Field Ambulance at Maidstone and 3/2nd West Lancs. Field Ambulance at Wye.	
	20/12/15		Sanitary Officer inspected prospective billets at Wingham, Elmstone and Preston and deemed not advisable to move troops in.	
	22/12/15.		A.D.M.S. inspected personnel etc. 3/2nd West Lancs. Field Ambulance at Canterbury.	

Canterbury,
8th January, 1916.

J. Schinler Cpt. R.A.M.C.(T)
for. A.D.M.S. 57th (West Lancs.) Division.

Confidential.

War Diary
of
Canl Units 57th (West Lancs) Divn.

From 1st Jany 1916 to 31st Jany 1916.

Army Form C. 2118

WAR DIARY
or
INTELLIGENCE SUMMARY

(Erase heading not required.)

Instructions regarding War Diaries and Intelligence Summaries are contained in F. S. Regs., Part II. and the Staff Manual respectively. Title Pages will be prepared in manuscript.

Place	Date	Hour	Summary of Events and Information	Remarks and references to Appendices
Canterbury.	1/1/1916.		Telegram from Reception, Wye reporting case of Epidemic Cerebro-Spinal Fever, all communications were carried out by this office. all Home Service men of 3/2nd W.L. Field Amblce. reported to Provisional Battalion.	
"	2/1/1916.		Divisional Sanitary Officer visited Wye with Medical Officer from Chatham.	
"	3/1/1916.		Patient Cerebro-Spinal died, did not belong to this Division.	
"	4/1/1916.		Travelling Medical Board reported to this Division. A case of sudden death from Pulmonary Embolism occurred.	
"	11/1/1916.		G.O.C. 57th Division inspected 2/3rd Wessex Field Ambulance at Maidstone.	
"	13/1/1916.		D.D.M.S. Central Force and A.D.M.S. 57th Division inspected 2/3rd Wessex Field Ambulance and Hospital. Also messing centres 172nd Infantry Brigade at Maidstone. G.O.C. 57th Division inspected 2/2nd Wessex Field Ambulance at Canterbury.	
"	24/1/1916.		A.D.M.S. ordered to hold himself in readiness to proceed overseas as A.D.M.S. 55th Division.	
"	27/1/1916.		A.D.M.S. ordered to report at General Headquarters, France on 31/1/1916.	
"	31/1/1916.		A.D.M.S. proceeded overseas from the Division.	

Canterbury,
7th February, 1916.

J. Edwston
Captain R.A.M.C. T.
acting
D.A.D.M.S. 57th (West Lancs.) Division.

Confidential

War Diary
of
D.M.S. 5th (West Lancs) Division
from 1st Feby 1916 to 29th Feby 1916.

Feb. 1916

Army Form C. 2118

WAR DIARY
or
INTELLIGENCE SUMMARY

(Erase heading not required.)

Instructions regarding War Diaries and Intelligence Summaries are contained in F. S. Regs., Part II. and the Staff Manual respectively. Title Pages will be prepared in manuscript.

Place	Date	Hour	Summary of Events and Information	Remarks and references to Appendices
Canterbury	11/2/16.		Death from Pneumonia reported by 2/2nd Wessex Field Ambulance. Man from 2/7th Liverpool Regt.	J.E.
"	16/2/16.		D.D.M.S., Central Force and Sanitary Officer 2nd Army visited Thanington Hutments with reference to a report that drainage from Camp was polluting Canterbury Water Supply. Arranged with Sanitary Officer 2nd Army to carry out tests. Also inspected Ersham House and Nackington Reception Hospital, advised strongly transfer of Hospital to Ersham, to be carried out as early as possible. All recommendations carried out or in process of being so.	J.E.
"	21/2/16.		Case of Enteric Fever reported from Reception Hospital, careful enquiry as to source gave no clue.	J.E.
"	22/2/16.		Thorough investigation of sanitary conditions of unit, from which case of Enteric was received	J.E.
"	24/2/16.		Weather very wintry, two days snow fall. At 11-15 a.m. message received from Divisional Headquarters that a period of vigilance was to commence and last until further orders. Everything was prepared for movements of Medical Details in case of emergency.	J.E.
"	25/2/16.		At Great Chart a civilian died of of Cerebro-Spinal Meningitis. Four soldiers billeted in house were isolated and throats swabbed, two found to be positive and two negative. Isolated accordingly.	J.E.
"	29/2/16.		Period of vigilance still being observed.	J.E.
			Average daily admittance to Hospital for Division for month of February - 18.1 Daily percentage of sick for Division. - 1 Infectious Cases for month of February. - 6 Percentage of fatal accidents. - Nil.	

Canterbury,

7th March, 1916.

J. Edwin

Captain R.A.M.C. T.
A/D.A.D.M.S. 57th (West Lancs.) Division.